Christmas 2003
from Brian/Cathy

Sylvia Cooks
SONORAN
STYLE

BY SYLVIA ABRIL

SYLVIA COOKS SONORAN STYLE

Published by Un Mujer, Inc, dba

Sylvia's La Canasta
5502 N. 7th Avenue
Phoenix, Arizona 85013

www.sylviasfiesta.com

ISBN 0-9704159-3-1

Printed in South Korea
First Edition

Written by: Sylvia Abril

Co-Authored by: Jill Van Dierendonck

Cover and Interior Design by: Christy A. Moeller-Masel

Edited by: Toni Caiola

DEDICATION

This cookbook is dedicated to my parents, Richard "Wero" Abril and Carmen Abril Lopez, who taught me to be creative and authentic in my cooking, business and life.

My father's self-developed "throw it together with flavor" cooking skills and dedication to his family and work were early and constant inspirations to me. My mother's intuitive business skills, her unending faith in God, and her prayers for all her children and grandchildren are the guiding lights of my life.

To both of you, I owe who I am today. Thank you, Dad and Mom.

ACKNOWLEDGEMENTS

This book is a tribute to my family, friends, customers, business associates and most of all, my Lord.

My family has built an outstanding reputation and loyal following by preparing and serving authentic, fresh and delicious Mexican foods. I've tried to take all I've learned from my parents and siblings and put it to work for me in my business. I have fond and vivid childhood memories filled with tortilla flour dust, hand-cut pork and piquant chiles. The work day in my family's butcher shop, grocery store, take-out tamale/tortilla shop, and restaurants began very early, and often didn't end until late in the evening. My sisters, brother and I would get up in the wee hours of the morning to shape and cook tortillas for local Valley restaurants, attend school, and then return to the restaurant to wait on customers before we completed our homework. Our parents instilled a strong work ethic in us – and also made work fun with contests to see who could make the fastest tortillas, tamales or burritos. We timed everything for speed, and measured everything for perfection. Often, I dreamed about tortillas and tamales in my sleep, and vowed I wouldn't be in the restaurant business when I was ready to make a career choice

for myself. Then, of course, I remembered one of the lessons my parents taught me: Work has to be fun. Now, I can't imagine doing anything as enjoyable and rewarding as making and serving delicious Mexican foods for many, many people to enjoy every day.

I owe my sisters and brother a great deal of gratitude for where I am today. They had a chance to help determine my fate, and voted to let me out of the family business "umbrella" several years ago. A special thanks to my sisters Diane and Josie, who came through again for me. I love you with all my heart for being there and cheering me on to success. Thank you all.

Coming from a "mom and pop" family business background, I know firsthand the sacrifices we as children made as our parents worked to feed and clothe us. Our family was large – seven children in all – and my parents worked very hard to provide for us. As a single mother of two, I see my children having to make similar sacrifices as they grow up – enabling me to fulfill obligations to my career and business. There were too many times I sent my daughter to school in a taxi because I was short of help and could not close the restaurant…and when she slept on a cot late at night in the back

kitchen as we made tamales for the next day. My young son practically lives in the restaurant office, and although I've added a couple amenities for him (cable TV and a basketball court out in back), I know our restaurant hours are still long. Nina and Matthew – you are my super cheerleaders, and I'll never be able to thank you enough for all your support and sacrifice. I love you.

Friends may come and go for a time in our lives, but there are some you will always remember. A special person who made a difference in my life was Irv Shuman, a sweet, older gentleman who saw potential in my small, obscure restaurant. This man invited me to lunch one day, and helped me see some possibilities I could not have discovered on my own. He helped me shape these ideas into reality. This was my second break in life, and to him I owe a great big hug and thanks. Thank you, Mr. Shuman.

A very special mention is also due Armando Delgadillo, my friend for life, for providing moral support and business guidance when I needed it. Thank you, Nando.

I've been blessed with a terrific team of employees in my business – and I owe each and every individual a great deal of gratitude for the good food and good business we've created. Thank you all for following the cooking methods and customer service policies I set forth. To Mario Ybarra, my general manager, and all my current employees: Keep up the good work! A special thanks to Juana Guarrero, my tamalera y major cocinera, for the last 10 years. Muchas gracias a todos!!

I owe a tremendous amount of gratitude to my **Sylvia's La Canasta** patrons – from people who live and work in the neighborhoods near my restaurants on 38th Avenue/Indian School Road and 7th Avenue/Missouri in Phoenix…to those planning small and large fiestas and choosing to serve specialties from my catering menus…to customers who read a review and decide to stop by for a quick, traditional Mexican plate…to my growing network of online customers looking to serve authentic Mexican dishes in their homes…and now to readers and cooking enthusiasts who have asked for this book. I say gracias, and buenas salud, felicidad y fortuna.

Thank you, too, my friends and family. You've kept me going during the rough times and the good times – whether it was sending me new customers, involving me in new business ventures, or working right alongside me in the kitchen. You were there whenever I needed you, and I've had plenty of those times. Thanks to the entire Abril and Salazar families; Bob and Lolita Knox; Ramon and Nancy Canniquez; Andrew Gomez; George Chavez; Ray and Ernestine Arvisu and my ex, Gary and his father, Tony Valenzuela. Thank you all!

TABLE OF CONTENTS

FAVORITOS DE LA FAMILIA (FAMILY FAVORITES)

INTRODUCTION

Flavorful food has been in my heart and soul – and yes, on my taste buds – for as long as I can remember. At a very early age I developed a love for the distinctive, fresh ingredients my parents and grandparents used in creating flavorful Mexican meals at home. While working alongside my parents in our family-owned market, (which included a butcher shop and later our first tamale/tortilla shop – the Original La Canasta Restaurant) I gained an appreciation for preparing Sonoran dishes customers would come back for time and again. From my family's entrepreneurial spirit and success, I learned the restaurant and food service business from the inside out. Growing up, my day began at 4 a.m., hand stretching tortillas before school, and returning after school to serve burritos and tacos to customers from our restaurant's walk-up counter.

Friends and patrons have asked me repeatedly over the years to share my food preparation secrets…to provide them with the "secret" ingredient that makes my Sylvia's Chicken Fiesta, Menudo and Chorizo unlike any found elsewhere.

I've always been humbled by these requests – and like many other chefs and restaurateurs – fully aware how much work is involved in teaching techniques and authoring recipes home chefs can successfully use to re-create their favorite restaurant dishes. I've also always wanted to fulfill these requests – but at the right time. I finally decided the time was right for *Sylvia Cooks Sonoran Style* – and that I would make the time to create a cookbook I was truly proud of. I've worked on the recipes for months – choosing a list of family favorites and dishes that are requested most often in my restaurant, until I came up with those that had just the right mix; experimenting with the proper proportions of ingredients (creating Sylvia's Chicken Fiesta and flan for a family of four is a bit different than making these dishes for a 40-person catered party!); and trying to add an extra dash of *sabor* to each with notes and stories I could only share with you if we were in the kitchen together, sipping a café de olla and preparing Green Corn Tamales for our Christmas posada.

I hope you enjoy cooking alongside me. I cherish the opportunity to share a part of my heritage, my passion, my life with you through these recipes, and I hope you find joy in preparing flavorful, festive Sonoran food and drinks for your family's table.

Gracias, amigas y familia.

Sylvia Abril
2003

MY FAMILY STORY: GENERATIONS OF GOOD COOKS FILL THE KITCHEN

by Sylvia Menchaca

Step into **Sylvia's La Canasta Restaurant** and your senses immediately tell you a lot about the food you're about to enjoy. Your eyes fill quickly with colorful hues of red, yellow, orange, violet, teal and green around the restaurant – just some of the vibrant colors that stand out so easily against a low desert landscape. Your ears pick up kaleidoscope-like sounds from the dining area: patrons discussing business, others engaged in lunchtime chatter, families sharing stories over dinner plates. Your taste buds are awakened by the distinctive smell of chiles, fresh-cooked tortillas, soups bursting with blended flavors, grilled meats.

Customers experience similar sensations when visiting any of the Abril family food establishments.

I have so many vivid memories of my parents, Richard "Wero" Abril and Carmen Abril Lopez, creating such wonderful food – food that people couldn't find just anywhere. Their cooking and their entrepreneurial spirit influenced me, my brother and my sisters so much. I guess it's just natural that we grew up to be in the business ourselves. All seven of us grew up working alongside our parents. We made tortillas, worked the kitchen making dad's famous burritos and mom's celebrated recipes, waited on customers, and even helped with the bookkeeping. Dad and Mom taught us the trade from the inside out.

Everything I know about the food business I learned from them…and the success I'm enjoying is due to their hard work, skills and inspiration.

My dad, Richard "Wero" Abril, was a butcher by trade, and also had experience working in a tortilla factory. He worked for Herseth Meat Packing Company in Phoenix before purchasing Linden Grocery Store with my mother. Running the small market convinced my parents they enjoyed owning their own business, and they soon purchased a small take-out food store, Rico's Tamale and Tortilla Shop. Everything on the menu was prepared from scratch, and as soon as we were old enough to stir large pots of sauce and stretch tortillas, we were added to the cooking team.

Our parents would develop the recipes and then teach us how to cook them. Dad was a man who loved to cook, and also someone who loved to have a good time. I will never forget the time he made a Polish sausage burrito – with jalapeño salad (which was pico de gallo before we knew it by that name), cheese and red chile sauce. It was an instant family favorite, and something our customers would order whenever they got the chance. It became so popular the *Arizona Republic* wrote about how Dad came up with the idea and recipe.

When my father died in 1974, Mom mourned deeply, but also showed resounding strength in carrying on with the family-built business by inspiring her children to face life's difficulties with resolve and passion. She has – and is – shaping generations of cooks and business leaders. Her seven children include daughters Linda Rios, Josie Ippolito, Diane Mendoza, Leticia Abril, Lydia Abril and me, and one son, Richard Abril. Mom is the matriarch in our family. All my siblings own their own restaurants or manage the family-owned tortilla factory, La Canasta Tortillas, and related enterprises. Her grandchildren and great-grandchildren will all be learning the family's culinary traditions as well.

The La Canasta family:
Sylvia's La Canasta Restaurant
Fiesta Catering Service
Sylvia's Fresh Mexican Food Products
Original La Canasta Restaurant
La Canasta Mexican Food Products
Lydia's La Canasta Restaurant
Richard's La Canasta Restaurant
La Canasta Capitolio Restaurant

SONORAN STYLE COOKING...
FROM MY KITCHEN TO YOURS

The recipes I've included in this book are derived from my family's table and from the busy kitchens in our family restaurants. I learned the cooking techniques and food preparation processes from watching my grandmothers, working alongside my parents, and from managing our family's restaurants. As I was growing up, I don't remember using a particular name or description to identify the food we created. It was simply "Mexican food." During the last decade or so, the term "Sonoran style" has come to be widely used to describe the flavorful, fresh – dare I say traditional – cooking I grew up with.

I'm proud to use the term to describe my menu favorites. The cuisine of the northern region of Mexico – specifically the state of Sonora, Mexico (which shares a border with Arizona) – influenced many of the dishes we prepare regularly in our restaurants. Many of the spices we use and sell come from indigenous plants grown in this area. My grandmother, Maria Salazar, who has lived in Sonora all her life, is the matriarch of the family businesses and the true Sonoran chef in our family. My grandparents played a very important role in all our lives, and they helped immensely with the success of the businesses.

Garcia's Mexican Restaurant was the first of her family's restaurants, and this business paved the way for my own family's businesses (the La Canasta family of restaurants and purveyors) and other acclaimed family restaurants (including Manuel's Mexican Restaurant, Popo's and Julio's G. Chains) to open their doors.

Many of the favorite dishes served in our family's restaurants today were developed in Grandma Maria's kitchen years ago – recipes distinctive in character, but always prepared in a similar style. The style was synonymous with rich, flavorful sauces and spices. The recipes may seem labor-intensive to a chef who is first learning the time-honored techniques, but it takes time to achieve the authentic burst of flavor characteristic of Sonoran style cooking. However, with a little practice (and some of the tips I'm about to share), you can re-create these dishes easily – whether you're in charge of the weeknight cooking for your family or preparing a few special dishes for a patio party.

What is it that distinguishes Sonoran style cooking from other types of "Mexican" or "Southwest" or "Tex-Mex" cuisine? I believe it's all in the sauces and spices.

In this book I describe how to make many of the distinctive, traditional Sonoran sauces: red chile sauce, green chile sauce, ranchero sauce, tamale chile and Salsa Fresca (probably one of the most popular sauces). Not surprisingly, fresh chiles play a central role in many of the dishes and recipes – as do flavorful spices. Fresh chiles often used in Sonoran style cooking include jalapeños, green chiles, chile tepins, crushed chiles and New Mexico chile pods. Popular produce items include cilantro, mint, green onions, tomatoes, yellow onions, limes, lemons, tomatillos and avocados. Traditionally, we do not use smoked chiles (such as chipotles) in our recipes – although these are a popular component of many "southwestern" dishes today. The spices we use are usually dried; rarely do we use fresh garlic or other fresh aromatics. The flavor that bursts from Sonoran style dishes develops in the simmering process. It's an important component to our cooking – and a process that cannot be rushed.

Inside *Sylvia Cooks Sonoran Style* you'll find recipes for many of my restaurant patrons'

favorite menu items – plus dishes my family requests over and over. You'll discover how to create tasty appetizers, soups, entrees and desserts. You'll learn how to put together complete meals, dishes you'll enjoy preparing for a special gathering, even how my red chile sauce can make tonight's sautéed chicken breast something special.

Most, if not all, of the ingredients listed in this cookbook are readily available in your local market or grocery – but I do recommend you purchase the spices direct from *Sylvia's Fresh Mexican Foods* to create that special and distinct Sonoran flavor. Please visit my Web site: *www.sylviasfiesta.com* where you may purchase a variety of my specially designed spice mixes.

I hope you enjoy re-creating the recipes in *Sylvia Cooks Sonoran Style*. You'll find the food delicious and flavorful, easy to prepare and pleasing to share with family and friends.

Buen provecho!

SONORAN FLAVORS
"SIMPLE INGREDIENTS, TECHNIQUES FROM THE HEART"

My style of Sonoran cooking does not require a restaurant license or culinary degree to achieve delicious results. My recipes are based on simple Mexican food preparation techniques and procedures. With a little guidance you'll be able to successfully prepare these satisfying dishes in your home for family and friends. In time, you will add or take away spices or ingredients and define your own style of Sonoran cooking. I won't be offended as this happens – in fact I encourage home chefs to experiment with and refine my recipes to make their own.

The ingredients listed with each recipe in this cookbook are limited, and should be readily available in your local grocery or market. You may be fortunate enough to find fresh chiles seasonally (be sure to purchase chiles that are shiny and firm) – along with home-grown tomatoes, onions, squash and citrus. Load up your market basket when this produce is at its freshest! Dried spices are easy to use and store. They do, however, lose some flavor over time. If it's been a while since you refreshed your spice pantry, stock up on new jars of spices and herbs. To ensure the distinct flavors of Sylvia's true Sonoran dishes, purchase the authentic Sonoran Spice Kit used in her restaurant at *www.sylviasfiesta.com*. You may have to ask your butcher for help with some of the cuts of meat I suggest, as your market may label or package cuts differently than I'm accustomed. Also, with most recipes you may substitute beef, pork, chicken and seafood to suite your tastes and diet (or what you have in your refrigerator) fairly easily.

To further help with menu preparation I've included a "shopping list" with each recipe. These lists identify all the ingredients and pantry items you'll need to prepare each recipe. No more mid-recipe trips to the market for a forgotten ingredient!

INGREDIENTS AND COOKING METHODS

CHILES, SPICES AND OTHER INGREDIENTS

You'll find chiles with unusual names, in vibrant colors and with varying degrees of heat in your local grocery. Sometimes this wide selection can be overwhelming to the novice Sonoran or Mexican cook…but don't despair; you'll only need to look for three or four varieties for my recipes. Listed below are the chiles that will be used in my Sonoran Recipes……Let's Get Started!

JALAPEÑO

Jalapeños are a common chile readily available year-round in most of your local supermarkets. Known to be one of the hotter peppers available, the jalapeño is also very widely used in many recipes today. It's

typically 3 inches long and 2 inches wide. This fiery pepper is used in most of our Sonoran recipes.

CHILE GÜERITOS- YELLOW HOTS

Yellow hots are similar in size but not in flavor to the jalapeños. The chile Güero has it's own distinct flavor. This chile also can be found in most supermarkets.

GREEN CHILES FOR ROASTING

The most common of all chiles is the long green chile. There are 2 varieties available. The most commonly used variety is the Anaheim green chile. The flavor is milder than, and not as hot as its counterpart, being the New Mexico Hatch green chile. Depending upon your preferred heat level, you can determine which one you would prefer to use in my recipes.

PREPARING ROASTED PEELED GREEN CHILES

The purpose of roasting the green chiles is to peel away the outer skin leaving the pulp and richness to use in recipes. We have given you four options to accomplish this. They are listed in the sequence that will yield the most flavorful results.

Roasting Method

Lightly brush fresh green chiles with vegetable oil and place in the broiler section of your oven. Turn the chiles for even roasting. The chile skin will become lightly charred and blistered. When chiles are roasted, place in a plastic bag to sweat, causing the skin to soften thus making it easy for peeling.

Frying Method

Heat 1 - 2 cups of oil in hot skillet. Fry chiles until golden brown; remove, and set on a plate with a paper towel to soak up the oil. When chiles are fried, place in plastic bag to sweat.

Water Boiling Method

Boil in water until the skin is easy to peel off the chile.

Store Method

Purchase canned green chiles that are already roasted and peeled from your local supermarket (the easiest method).

DRY RED CHILE PODS – FOR CHILE DE SARTA

Dried red chiles are the authentic chiles used in Sonoran style Mexican food cuisine. They generally need to be re-hydrated before using. This reddish, fruity and mild tasting sun dried chile is frequently used in my Sonoran recipes. They are often sold in the Mexican section of supermarkets (as dried chile pods).

PREPARING CHILE DE SARTA

In the Sonoran cuisine, Chile de Sarta is the chile paste base we use in a variety of the restaurant recipes.

3 ounce package of mild or hot dry red chiles
4 cups of water

The first step in preparing the dry chile pods is to rinse them off. They are usually dried in the sun and exposed to the outdoor elements, and we recommend you rinse them before using. Break the tails off and shake out the seeds. Don't worry if the

chiles break up. Discard the seeds and tails.

In a medium sauce pan, add the cleaned chiles and water. Bring to a boil, reduce the temperature and simmer for 45 - 60 minutes or until the chiles are soft and pliable.

Do not add additional water. Transfer the softened chiles to a blender, add $1/2$ cup of the chile stock (liquid) and blend until smooth. This recipe should yield about 2 cups of Chile de Sarta.

OTHER FAVORITE DRIED CHILES
*Chile Tepin • Crushed red peppers (hot &
mild) • Chile powder (hot & mild) • Chile Arbol*

Dried chiles are found in a variety of my
Sonoran dishes. You can find them in the
Mexican Food or Produce sections of your
local supermarket.

BROWNING THE FLOUR – ROUX
$^1/_2$ cup of oil or lard
1 cup of flour

In a heavy skillet heat oil/lard. Using a wire
whip, gently add flour to hot oil whipping until
smooth. Brown flour until light tan in color.
Yield $^3/4$ cup.

Preparing stocks (See Flautas recipe for
pollo, Chile Rojo for beef and Chile de
Puerco for pork).

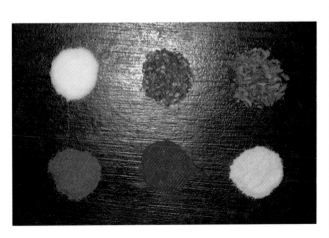

COMMONLY USED
SONORAN SPICES
*Granulated garlic • Whole leaf oregano •
Ground cumin • Cilantro flakes*

You can order all of these, plus more, through
Sylvia's Fresh Mexican Foods
1-866-564-2769
www.sylviasfiesta.com

SALSA FRESCA
A hearty salsa to always have on hand

PICO DE GALLO
Dad's fresh jalapeño and tomato salad

GUACAMOLE
A delicious avocado dip

POLLO QUESADILLAS
Chicken cheese crisps to please a crowd

MARISCOS CON ARROZ
Seafood served with rice

"T he English translation for Salsa Fresca is fresh salsa. My version of the recipe calls for canned tomatoes and canned green chiles, however. Using canned products allows you to use the juices the tomatoes and green chiles are packed in; these juices produce very robust flavors you're about to experience. To experience the Salsa Fresca's truest flavors, refrigerate for 24 hours before serving. This allows the flavors to come together and fully develop. Prepare this recipe once a week and have fresh salsa to enjoy all week long – if your family can resist eating it in one day!

GROCERY LIST

Yellow hots
Yellow onion
Jalapeño
Can of whole peeled
  tomatoes in tomato juice
Cilantro
Crushed chile peppers
Cumin
Granulated garlic
Salt
Green chiles

Salsa Fresca

SALSA FRESCA PREPARATION
3 fresh yellow hots, diced coarsely
3 tablespoons yellow onion, diced coarsely
2 fresh jalapeños, diced coarsely
16 oz. can whole peeled tomatoes in tomato juice
$1/2$ cup diced green chiles (roasted or canned),
  cut into $1/4$-inch pieces
$1^1/2$ tablespoon fresh minced cilantro

SPICES
$1^1/2$ teaspoons salt
$1/2$ teaspoon crushed chile peppers
$1/4$ teaspoon cumin
$1/2$ teaspoon granulated garlic

1 Prepare the vegetables. Combine the yellow hot chiles, yellow onion and jalapeños in a blender and pulse until the chiles are minced finely. Do not over pulse.

2 Drain juice from the canned tomatoes and reserve juice in medium bowl. Cut tomatoes into quarters and transfer to blender. Pulse five times. Do not over pulse. Chunky is what we want. Transfer tomatoes into the bowl of tomato juice. Use a spoon to mix well.

3 Add the spices, green chiles and fresh cilantro, and continue to mix until all ingredients are combined. Transfer the Salsa Fresca to a storage container, cover and refrigerate 24 hours. Yield $2^1/2$ cups.

SERVING SUGGESTION
Use this salsa for dipping chips, or to top breakfast, lunch or dinner dishes.

Pico de Gallo

INGREDIENTS

2 cups $1/2$-inch diced tomatoes
2 tablespoons fine cilantro leaves, minced
3 tablespoons yellow onion, minced fine
4 tablespoons fresh jalapeños (2), minced
2 tablespoons fresh boiled jalapeños peeled (1), minced
1 tablespoon fresh green onions, chopped fine
2-3 tablespoons fresh lemon juice

SPICES

$3/4$ teaspoon salt, to taste
$1/8$ teaspoon cumin
$1/2$ teaspoon granulated garlic

1 Combine all ingredients together in a medium-size bowl and mix well. Add spices and salt to taste.

"*This is truly a fresh salsa made with fresh ingredients that can be served right away. This tangy salsa was introduced to me by my father who I always thought created it. We didn't call it Pico de Gallo at the time but 'Dad's Fresh Jalapeño Salad.' For short, we called it Jala Salad. When I was growing up, the customers would order a burrito with Jala Salad in it. In the past 10 years the name has changed to Pico de Gallo.*"

SERVING SUGGESTION
You can eat this salsa with just about anything: beans, chips, tacos, tostadas. You can mix this to make guacamole. A favorite of mine is to serve it with Menudo.

Makes 2 cups.

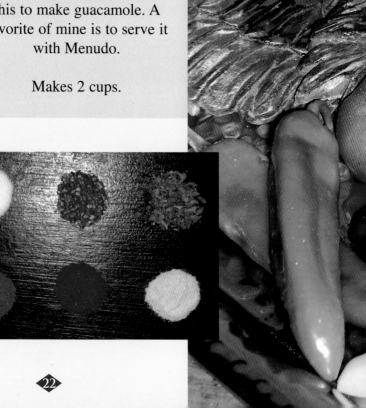

GROCERY LIST

Tomatoes
Cilantro leaves
Yellow onion
Jalapeño peppers
Green onions
Fresh lemon juice
Salt
Cumin
Garlic

Guacamole

PREPARING THE GUACAMOLE

2 medium avocados (ripe)
1 small tomato, diced fine
2 roasted jalapeños, minced fine
2 tablespoons fresh cilantro, minced
2 tablespoons yellow onions, minced
2 tablespoons sour cream
1 tablespoon fresh lemon juice

SPICES
$3/4$ teaspoon salt, to taste
$1/2$ teaspoon garlic
$1/8$ teaspoon cumin

"This delicious dip has long been made for dipping with tortilla chips. Then, when chimichangas became a popular restaurant dish, this delicious avocado dip became a natural topping. Most Mexican restaurants today serve their trademark chimichanga with guacamole and sour cream on top. You can serve guacamole with almost all Mexican dishes."

❶ Cut avocado lengthwise. Use a spoon to scoop out the pulp of the avocado and place into a bowl. Use a fork to mash the pulp.

❷ Add tomatoes, roasted jalapeños, cilantro and onion to the avocado pulp. Mix well.

❸ Add the spices, sour cream and lemon juice.

❹ Refrigerate or serve immediately.

GROCERY LIST
Avocados
Tomatoes
Jalapeños
Cilantro
Yellow onion
Sour cream
Lemon juice
Salt
Garlic
Cumin

"*This is a great appetizer dish to serve when guests are over or during the festive holiday season.*"

Pollo Quesadilla
Chicken Cheese Crisp

PREPARING THE POLLO QUESADILLAS FILLING

This filling can be made one day in advance and refrigerated until you're ready to prepare the quesadillas. In this quesadilla recipe, you'll use about $1/2$ of the filling you prepare. The remaining filling can be refrigerated for later use.

$1^1/2$ lbs. skinless, boneless chicken
(using both dark and light meat)
$1/4$ teaspoon granulated garlic
$1/4$ teaspoon salt
$4^1/2$ cups water

❶ In a small stock pot bring to a boil chicken, salt and garlic. Skim off the impurities and fat that float to the top. Reduce heat and simmer on medium-high temperature until chicken is cooked through. The stock should reduce to 4 cups. Skim off excess fat. Remove chicken, drain broth (reserve in stock pot), and set aside. When chicken is cooled, remove and discard bones. Shred cooked chicken into 1- inch pieces. Set aside.

1 tablespoon butter/margarine
$1/4$ cup green onions, cut into $3/4$-inch pieces
$1/4$ cup roasted green chiles, diced into $1/4$-inch pieces
$1/4$ cup yellow onion, cut into $1/2$-inch pieces
1 small/medium-size tomato, cut into $1/2$-inch pieces
1 chicken bouillon cube
4 cups of chicken broth

GROCERY LIST

One dozen flour tortillas
Cheddar cheese
Green onion
Tomatoes
Skinless boneless chicken
Granulated garlic
Salt
Butter/margarine
Roasted green chiles
Chicken bouillon cubes
Chicken broth
Yellow onions
Cilantro flakes
Black pepper
Cumin

SPICES
$1/4$ tablespoon cilantro flakes
$1/2$ teaspoon granulated garlic
$1/2$ teaspoon pepper
$1/4$ teaspoon cumin
$1/2$ teaspoon salt, to taste

❷ In medium skillet over medium-high heat, sauté onions, green onions and roasted chiles in margarine or butter until soft. Add tomatoes and continue to sauté until tomatoes are cooked.

❸ In small stock pot, bring to a boil 4 cups chicken broth.

Add the sautéed vegetables, spices and bouillon cube. Reduce heat to medium. Add shredded chicken and simmer over medium-high heat for 20 minutes. Remove from heat and let cool. Using wire sieve, drain the broth. Press the chicken into the sieve to extract as much of the liquid as possible. Refrigerate the quesadilla filling for 15 minutes. You should have enough filling for 12 eight-inch size quesadillas. Reserve chicken broth for another use.

QUESADILLAS PREPARATION
1 dozen 8-inch La Canasta flour tortillas
2$^{1}/_{2}$ lbs. grated cheddar cheese
1 cup fresh green onions, diced $^{1}/_{4}$-inch fine
3 cups tomatoes, diced $^{1}/_{4}$-inch cube
2-3 cups pollo (shredded chicken)
                topping for quesadillas

Quesadillas can be folded or prepared open, served cut up like pizza.

To prepare open quesadillas: Preheat griddle to medium temperature. Place tortilla on griddle, sprinkle shredded cheese onto tortilla, spreading cheese lightly across the top of the tortilla. Use a rubber spatula to spread melted cheese evenly. Add shredded chicken, green onion and tomato filling. Lightly sprinkle more cheese on top. Allow the tortilla to cook until crisp on the bottom before removing.

To prepare folded quesadillas: Use only $^{1}/_{2}$ of the tortilla for the filling. Fold the other side of tortilla over the filled half. Flip quesadillas over from one side to the other until both sides of the quesadilla are toasted.

Using a pizza cuter, slice the quesadilla into 4-6 pieces.

Serve with freshly made guacamole, Sylvia's Salsa Picante, *Pico de Gallo* or *Salsa Fresca.*

"*During the festive holiday season many Mexican cooks would make a sign of the cross asking the Lord to bless the flavors and multiply the food. This dish is symbolic of the biblical scripture written in Matthew 14:17. European influences have inspired many creative dishes. This one I especially liked. I serve this dish as an appetizer when I have guests over.*"

GROCERY LIST

Long grain rice
Fresh green chilies
Olive oil
Whole milk
Chicken broth
Salt
Black pepper
Butter/margarine
Chile de Arbol, crushed
Garlic cloves
Fresh portabella mushrooms
Raw peeled shrimp with tails
Octopus
Avocados
Limes
Clams (optional)

Mariscos con Arroz
Seafood with Rice

RICE PREPARATION

1 1/2 cups long grain rice
1 cup fresh green chiles, seeded and cut into 1/2-inch pieces
1/3 cup olive oil
1 1/2 cup whole milk
2 3/4 cups chicken broth, or water with three chicken bouillon cubes for flavor

SPICES

1/4 teaspoon salt, to taste
1/4 teaspoon pepper

❶ Soak rice in hot water for 15 minutes. Drain in mesh sieve, rinse in cold water until water runs clear.

❷ Heat oil in large skillet over medium-high temperature. Add rice and fry until color of rice is bone white. Add green chiles and continue to fry until rice color is very light yellow and chiles are softened.

❸ In a sauce pan, bring to a boil the milk and chicken broth. Add salt and pepper. Remove from heat and pour into the rice skillet. Bring to a brisk boil, then reduce temperature to low and simmer, covered tightly, for 30 minutes. Remove from heat and let set covered for 20 minutes until rice finishes steaming.

SAUTEED MARISCOS PREPARATION

3 tablespoon butter or margarine
4 tablespoons extra virgin olive oil
1 tablespoon Chíle de Arbol, crushed
3 large cloves fresh garlic, chopped fine
1 1/2 cups fresh portabella mushrooms, cut in 1-inch pieces (6 oz. tray of fresh mushrooms, sliced)
1 package 51-60 raw peeled shrimp with tails
3/4 cup fresh cleaned octopus, cut into 1/2-inch pieces
1/2 cup clams (optional)
1 teaspoon salt

❹ Melt margarine or butter on a flat skillet. Add the olive oil. Reduce temperature to medium. Add the chiles and sauté about 2 minutes. Add the chopped garlic and sauté until soft. Add the mushrooms and continue to sauté for 2 minutes.

5 Add the octopus to the skillet of mushrooms and chiles and sauté for about 1 minute. Add thawed, rinsed shrimp to skillet and sauté until shrimp is firm, and pink/white in color. Add salt to taste.

6 Transfer steamed rice into a large pasta dish and top with the sautéed mariscos.

GARNISH
1 avocado, cut into slices
1 lime, sliced into wedges

Serve immediately. Makes 6-8 appetizer-size portions.

ALBONDIGAS
Mexican meatball soup

COCIDO
Vegetable beef soup (Mexican style)

MENUDO ROJO
Hominy beef tripe soup

"This hearty Mexican soup is great during the cold winter months...but we serve this delicious soup every day of the year at Sylvia's. It's best served with lemons, crushed red chile peppers and La Canasta flour or corn tortillas.

GROCERY LIST

Tomato juice
Beef short ribs
Yellow onion
Tomatoes
Cilantro
Garlic cloves
Mint leaves
Corn ears
Oregano
Cumin
Salt
Potatoes
Whole green chilies
Zucchini
Garbanzo beans
Celery
Carrots
Bay leaves
Granulated garlic

Cocido

Mexican-style vegetable beef soup

PREPARING THE BEEF STOCK/INGREDIENTS

12 cups water
$1/2$ cup tomato juice
5-6 beef short ribs
1 medium yellow onion, cut into 1-inch pieces
1 medium tomato, cut into 1-inch pieces
1 tablespoon minced cilantro
2 fresh whole garlic cloves
3 fresh whole mint leaves, tied together
2 medium ears of corn
    (about 6 inches long), cut into 4 pieces

1 Combine all of the above ingredients together in a large stock pot. Bring to a boil over high heat.

2 Reduce temperature to medium and add the following spices:
        1 pinch crushed oregano
        1 pinch cumin
        1 tablespoon salt, to taste

3 Continue to cook for additional $1^1/2$ hours.

PREPARING THE VEGETABLE STOCK/ INGREDIENTS

7 cups of water
3 medium potatoes (skin on),
    cut in 2-inch pieces (about 2 cups)
2 celery stalks, cut into 2-inch pieces
2 carrots, peeled and sliced $1/2$-inch thick
$3/4$ cup whole fresh green chilies,
    seeded, cut into $1/2$-inch pieces
1 whole zucchini, sliced in $1/2$-inch pieces

1 Combine all of the above ingredients together in a large stock pot. Bring to a boil, then reduce to medium temperature and cook for 30 minutes.

2 Gently transfer vegetables and stock to beef stock, and add the following spices:

1¹/2 tablespoon salt, to taste
1 tablespoon granulated garlic
¹/4 teaspoon cumin
2 bay leaves
1 12-oz. can garbanzo beans, drained

❸ Simmer for an additional 20 minutes.

SERVING SUGGESTION

Serve soup in a large soup tureen, garnishing with fresh minced cilantro and lemons.

Makes enough for 4-6 portions.

"I've heard the best Albondigas soup has its origins in the Mexican states of Sonora and Sinaloa. My grandmother, being from Sonora, prepared this soup plenty of times and I can say it's true. I can just see my grandmother right now, in her kitchen rolling the meatballs while we played around her. I still smell the aroma of the soup. Oh, what wonderful memories to have!"

GROCERY LIST

Tomatoes
Yellow onion
Carrots
Celery
Mint leaves
Butter/margarine
Granulated garlic
Salt
Chicken bouillon cubes
Whole oregano
Cumin powder
Lean ground beef
Eggs
Rice
Black pepper
All purpose flour
Green onion

Albondigas Soup
Mexican Meatball Soup

STOCK PREPARATION/INGREDIENTS
8 cups of water
1 medium tomatoes, cut into quarters
1/2 yellow onion, diced in 1/2-inch pieces
1 medium-size carrot, sliced in 1/4-inch rounds
1/2 cup celery, cut in 1/2-inch diagonal slices
2 fresh mint leaves
2 tablespoons butter/margarine

SPICES
1 tablespoon granulated garlic
2 teaspoons salt
2 chicken bouillon cubes
2 pinches of whole oregano, crushed between your fingers
1 1/2 teaspoons cumin powder

1 Combine in stock pot: water, tomatoes, yellow onions, carrots, celery, mint leaves and butter/margarine. Bring to a boil. Reduce the heat and add the spices. Continue to simmer for an additional 20 minutes. During this simmering time you can prepare the Albondigas.

PREPARING THE ALBONDIGAS/ INGREDIENTS
1 pound of lean ground beef
1 whole egg
1/4 cup rice (rinse with water until water runs clear)
3 tablespoons minced tomatoes
1 tablespoon minced green onion
1 tablespoon minced yellow onion

SPICES
1/2 teaspoon pepper, to taste
1/4 teaspoon cumin
1 teaspoon salt, to taste
1 teaspoon granulated garlic
1 tablespoon flour

① Mix all ingredients together in a large mixing bowl. The beef texture will be similar to meat loaf but stickier. Take about 2 tablespoons of the beef, place into the palm of your hand, and roll into a small two-inch size ball. Yield is about 25 Albondigas (meat balls).

② Now add the meatballs one at time to the simmering vegetable stock. Do not stir, or if you must, stir lightly. Simmer for an additional 30-40 minutes or until the meatballs are cooked through.

SERVING SUGGESTION

Serve Albondigas soup over Mexican rice.

Garnish with fresh minced cilantro and oregano.

Serve with La Canasta corn or flour tortillas.

"*Menudo is well known as a traditional holiday dish – and even better known as a cure for a hangover. For Christmas and New Year's celebrations it's customary to have a large pot of Menudo ready for your family and guests. It is served with fresh cilantro, chile tepin, whole oregano and fresh lemon wedges. At Sylvia's we serve Menudo every Saturday and Sunday for breakfast year-round.*"

GROCERY LIST
Beef tripe
Nixtamale (semi-cooked kernel corn)
Pata (fresh cow's feet)
Yellow onion
Fresh garlic
Lemons
Cilantro
Green onion
Oregano
Chile powder
    (hot or mild)
Salt
Chile de Sarta

Menudo Rojo
Red Menudo

MENUDO PREPARATION
6 lbs. beef tripe
4-8 lemons for cleaning and garnish
3 lbs. of nixtamale (par-cooked corn - hominy)
3 pieces of pata (beef feet)
10 quarts water (approximately)
1 large yellow onion
3 cloves fresh garlic, peeled
2 cups prepared Chile de Sarta (see page 16 for instructions)
Salt, oregano and chili powder (hot or mild) – all to taste

GARNISH
2 bunches cilantro, coarsely chopped
2-3 bunches green onions, diced in 1/4-inch pieces

CLEANING PROCESS FOR BEEF TRIPE

❶ Lay out the beef tripe on a cutting board, and trim off excess fat. Cut 2-3 lemons in half. Using fresh lemons, scrub beef tripe, squeezing juice onto tripe as you are cleaning. (Make sure the lemon juice has been spread over both sides.) Rinse well with cold water. Cut cleaned tripe into 2-inch square pieces. Rinse beef feet in cold water. Set aside.

❷ Rinse nixtamale under cold running water, removing skin from kernels. Set aside.

❸ In 12-quart stock pot, **layer ingredients in the following order** (this is essential to the cooking process): nixtamale, beef tripe, then beef feet. Do not mix or stir. Add water to within 2 inches of the top of the pot. Do not stir.

❹ Peel outer layer of skin from the yellow onion. Add this whole yellow onion and whole garlic cloves to the pot. Cook uncovered for 5 hours over medium-low heat. Check the water level occasionally, and replenish water as needed. Do not stir until the kernels are busted. When the kernels have burst, add the Chile de Sarta. Continue to cook for 15 minutes. Add optional spices (garlic powder, chile powder, oregano and salt) to taste. Stir well.

5 During the cooking process, prepare the garnish. Coarsely chop cilantro bunches, and place in a condiment bowl. Remove the tops of the green onions, peel away any excess skin, chop finely, and place in another condiment bowl.

SERVING SUGGESTIONS
Serve with crushed chiles, Pico de Gallo, toasted and buttered French rolls, corn tortillas or flour tortillas.

This recipe will yield 10-20 servings.

Special order unprepared Menudo Kits from:
Sylvia's La Canasta Restaurants
5502 North 7th Avenue
Phoenix, Az 85013 • (602) 242-4252

3824 West Indian School Road,
Phoenix, Az 85019 • (602) 269-2101

Sylvia's Fresh Mexican Foods
Toll free: (866) 564-2769

Sold in the following quantities:
$1/2$ Menudo recipe • (12 lbs. tripe)
Serves 20-40 • Requires a 32-quart pot

$1/4$ Menudo recipe • (6 lbs. tripe)
Serves 10-15 • Requires a 16-quart pot

FRIJOLES
Pinto beans

ARROZ
Mexican Rice

CALABACITAS CON QUESO
Summer squash with cheese and tomatoes

"Beans are a staple in Mexican cuisine, and they're served throughout Mexico as well as in Mexican restaurants in the United States. I often judge a restaurant on the flavor of the beans it serves. In our family restaurants, customers can rely on consistently delicious frijoles. This recipe is my home recipe."

Frijoles
Pinto beans

INGREDIENTS/PREPARATION
1 lb. pinto beans, washed and sorted
4 cups water
5 slices of bacon
1 green onion stalk
Salt, to taste

1 Spread the beans over a cutting board and clean beans of the debris and small rocks that usually accompany them. Rinse well.

2 In medium sauce pan add water, beans, bacon and green onion. Cook uncovered for $2^{1}/_{2}$ hours (until beans are tender), checking every 20-30 minutes for water level. Throughout cooking you will need to add warm water as it evaporates, keeping the level of water the same at all times. When beans are cooked, add salt to taste. Remove bacon from cooked beans and mince fine. Add minced bacon back to beans. Remove green onion and discard. You can eat the beans whole or you can mash them for refried beans (see below).

VARIATION: Add 1 lb. cooked chorizo to make a delicious chorizo bean soup.

Refried Beans

1 Drain bean juice and reserve for later. Transfer beans and minced bacon to KitchenAid mixer set to level one. Using the paddle attachment, mix the beans until they reach your desired texture (adding bean stock as necessary). Mashing can also be done by hand or with a hand-held mixer.

2 Serve immediately or refrigerate. To reheat, use a skillet with 1 teaspoon lard or oil and heat to your desired temperature.

Garnish with shredded cheddar cheese. Accompany with fresh flour or corn tortillas.

Makes 8 servings.

GROCERY LIST
Pinto Beans
Lard or oil for refrying
Bacon
Green onion stalk
Cheddar cheese

"*Rice and beans are the traditional side dishes served in nearly all Mexican restaurants and homes. Although they are just side dishes, they play a very important part in complementing the main entree.*"

Mexican Rice

RICE PREPARATION

$1^1/2$ cups white rice (rinse rice under running water
  until the water is clear)
4 tablespoons vegetable oil
2 tablespoons margarine
$1/4$ cup green onion, diced in $1/4$-inch pieces
$1/2$ cup yellow onion, diced in $1/4$-inch pieces
2 small tomatoes, diced in $1/2$-inch chunks
$1/4$ cup roasted green chiles, chopped fine
6 oz. canned tomato sauce
2 tablespoons fresh cilantro, chopped or dry cilantro flakes

SPICES

$1/2$ teaspoon cumin
1 teaspoon garlic
1 teaspoon pepper
2 chicken bouillon cubes
Salt to taste
2 cups chicken broth or water (if you're using water, add
  6-8 chicken bouillon cubes or chicken base for flavor)

1 Prepare the vegetables and set aside. In a large semi-deep skillet, heat the oil. Add rice, and stir until all rice grains are coated with oil. Fry rice, stirring intermittently, until it reaches a nice golden brown color.

2 In a small skillet, melt the margarine. Add yellow and green onions and sauté until soft. Add tomatoes, and continue to cook until soft. Add green chile and cook for 5 more minutes. Add sautéed vegetables to the browned rice, mixing all ingredients well. Add 2 cups of chicken broth, the tomato sauce, spices, bouillon cubes and salt to taste. Bring to a rapid boil, and cook for 3 minutes. Reduce heat and cook for 10 minutes. Reduce heat to medium-low, and cover the rice skillet with a lid. Do not stir. When broth is absorbed, tiny holes should appear in the surface of the rice. (This takes about 15-20 minutes over medium-low heat). Remove from heat.

GROCERY LIST

White rice
Vegetable oil
Margarine
Green onion
Yellow onion
Tomatoes
Tomato sauce
Roasted green chiles
Cilantro
Garlic
Cumin
Black pepper
Chicken bouillon cubes
Salt

SERVING SUGGESTIONS

Garnish with green onions, avocado and tomato wedges. You can serve rice as a side dish with all Mexican meals.

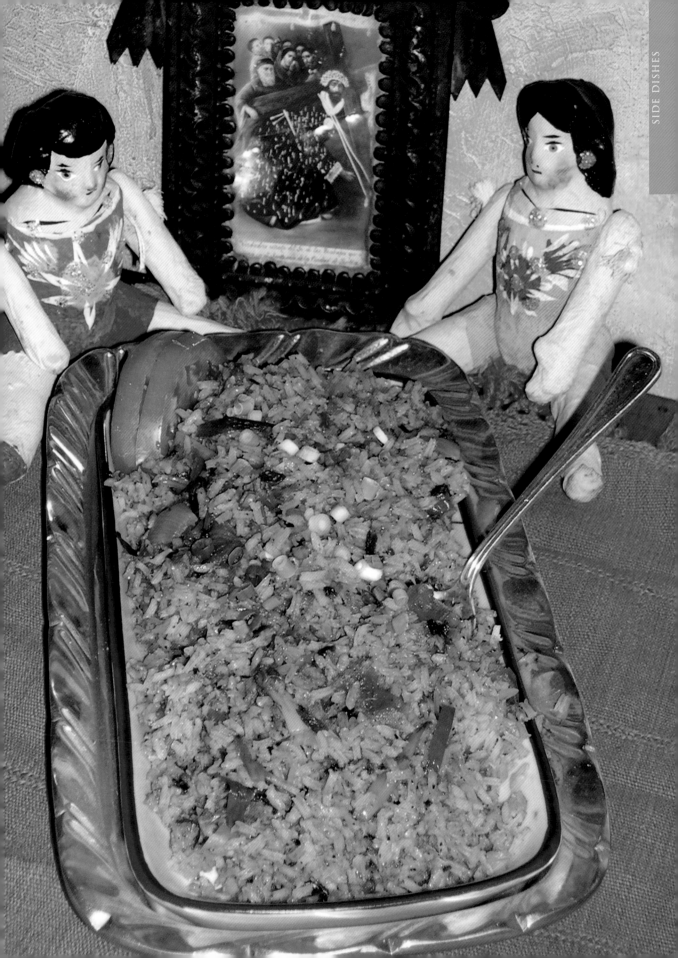

"*T*his was one of my favorite family recipes growing up. My mother would prepare calabacitas with steak dinners – as did her mother."

Zucchini, Sonoran Style

CALABACITAS PREPARATION
3 tablespoons butter or margarine
$1/2$ cup yellow onion, diced fine
2 small tomatoes, diced in $1/2$-inch pieces
3 large zucchini, cubed in 2-inch pieces
1 cup water
1 8 oz. can corn (do not drain)
$1/2$ teaspoon garlic
1 teaspoon salt
1 good pinch oregano
$1/4$ cup evaporated milk
$1/2$ cup grated cheese
   (Wisconsin cheddar or Monterey Jack)

❶ In a large skillet over medium heat, melt butter or margarine. Add onions and sauté until soft. Add tomatoes, and cook until soft. Stir in zucchini and continue to cook for 10 minutes. Add water, corn and spices. Simmer until zucchini is soft. Add milk and continue to cook for 5 more minutes. Sprinkle cheese over the dish right before serving.

Yield 4 servings.

GROCERY LIST
Zucchini
Tomatoes
Yellow onion
Canned corn
Butter or margarine
Granulated garlic
Dried oregano
Evaporated milk
Cheese

CHORIZO CON HUEVOS
Mexican sausage with eggs

HUEVOS RANCHEROS
Eggs served Mexican ranch style

CHILE RELLENO
Stuffed green chile deep fried in egg batter

"This recipe is a favorite in our family restaurants; we serve it every day for breakfast. You can mix chorizo with eggs, potatoes, cheese and onions to make a hearty breakfast burrito."

GROCERY LIST
Ground pork
Ground beef
Skinless pork sausage
New Mexico chile pods
Mild chili powder
Cumin
Granulated garlic
Salt
Crushed oregano
Crushed chile peppers
Vinegar
Eggs
Potatoes

Chorizo con Huevos
Eggs and Mexican Sausage

FRESH CHORIZO PREPARATION
3/4 lb. ground pork
1/4 lb. ground beef
12 oz. package of skinless pork sausage
(do not use sausage links)
1 1/2 cups Chile de Sarta
(see page 16 for preparation instructions)
1/4 cup mild chili powder

SPICES
1 teaspoon cumin
1 teaspoon granulated garlic
1 tablespoon salt
1 tablespoon whole oregano, crushed
2 tablespoons crushed chile peppers
1/4 cup vinegar

1 Using a KitchenAid mixer (set on level one) combine all three meats together and mix well. (If you prefer, you can mix these meats by hand in a medium bowl.) The texture will be very sticky – like dough. Add chili powder, and continue to mix until chili powder is dissolved. Add Chile de Sarta and continue to mix. Add spices, and mix an additional 5 minutes. Add the vinegar and incorporate well. (The vinegar is used to cure the combined meat products.)

2 Transfer the chorizo to a large glass bowl, cover with plastic wrap and refrigerate for 24 hours before cooking. This recipe will yield about 2 pounds of fresh chorizo, which can be stored in freezer bags and thawed in the refrigerator before use. I recommend cooking 6-8 eggs for each pound of cooked chorizo.

COOKING CHORIZO CON HUEVOS
Chorizo must always be cooked prior to adding eggs or other ingredients.

3 In a large skillet, add 1 tablespoon of oil and fry 1 lb. of chorizo until it resembles cooked ground beef. Add 6-8 whole eggs, folding into chorizo until cooked to your desired texture.

SERVING SUGGESTIONS
Serve with refried beans and La Canasta Tortillas. Garnish with Sylvia's Picante salsa.

This recipe will serve 3-4 people (3-4 burritos using 8- or 10-inch La Canasta flour tortillas).

"Huevos Ranchero is a popular Sunday brunch dish. This traditional, over-easy egg dish is served atop fresh, hot corn tortillas, topped with ranchero sauce and cheese. Served with beans and rice, this dish makes a delicious Mexican breakfast."

GROCERY LIST

Yellow onion
Jalapeño pepper
Green onion
Tomatoes
Butter/margarine
Chicken broth
Granulated garlic
Cumin
Dried oregano
Cilantro
Corn starch

Huevos Ranchero
Mexican Ranch Style Eggs

PREPARING THE RANCHERO SAUCE

1 medium yellow onion, cut in half and thinly sliced
1 fresh jalapeño, cut in half and thinly sliced
3-4 green onions, cut $^{1}/2$-inch long pieces (about $^{1}/2$ cup)
3 medium red ripe tomatoes, sliced in thin rounds
3 tablespoons butter or margarine
2 cups chicken broth
1 cup water

SPICES

$^{1}/2$ teaspoon garlic
$^{1}/4$ teaspoon cumin
1 small pinch oregano
1 tablespoon fresh cilantro, minced
Salt and pepper, to taste
2 tablespoons corn starch, mixed with a little water

1 Prepare the vegetables. In a medium skillet, heat the butter or margarine. Add yellow onions, jalapeños and green onions. Cook vegetables until soft and pale in color. Add tomatoes and stir. Cover and simmer, stirring often until the mixture resembles tomato paste. Add chicken broth, water and spices. Simmer for an additional 10 minutes over medium-high heat. Add fresh cilantro, reduce heat and simmer 10 minutes. Add corn starch mixture, using your discretion to thicken. Remove from heat and set aside.

PREPARING THE HUEVOS

8 eggs
8 fresh corn tortillas
$^{1}/2$ cup oil

2 Prepare a plate with paper towel lining to soak up oil from tortillas.

3 In medium skillet, heat half of the oil. Using tongs, dip tortilla into the hot oil (one at a time). Do not leave in the oil more than 2-4 seconds, just enough time to soften each tortilla. Place lightly fried tortillas on the lined plate to absorb excess oil.
(*Alternative to frying:* Place tortillas between dampened paper towels and heat for 10 seconds in microwave.)

 Place two corn tortillas on each serving plate before you start cooking the eggs. Fry eggs either over-easy or sunny-side up. Place cooked eggs atop lightly fried or softened corn tortillas. Cover (smother) the eggs/tortillas with the ranchero sauce. Sprinkle with grated cheese. Repeat until you have completed your plates. Garnish with finely chopped green onions.

SERVING SUGGESTIONS
• Refried Pinto beans as side dish
• Salsa and La Canasta flour tortillas

"*Relleno in Spanish means to stuff or fill. In this recipe we are stuffing the chiles with Wisconsin Cheddar or Monterey Jack cheese and frying them in an egg batter. There are many recipes available on different ways to prepare and stuff chiles. You can substitute the cheese with meat or chicken, and you can substitute the roasted green chiles for poblano chiles or roasted bell peppers. Rellenos are almost always served with a savory Relleno sauce on top.*"

GROCERY LIST
Eggs
Green onion
Yellow onion
Tomatoes
Jalapeño peppers
Margarine
Chicken stock
Chicken bouillon cubes
Crushed cumin powder
Garlic
Oregano
Salt
Cornstarch
Roasted green chiles de-seeded
Wisconsin cheddar cheese
    or Monterey Jack cheese
All-purpose flour

Chili Rellenos

PREPARING THE RELLENO SAUCE
1 cup green onions, cut into 1-inch pieces
1 medium yellow onion, cut in half and thinly sliced
1 medium tomato, cut in half and thinly sliced
1 jalapeño, cut in thin rings
2 tablespoons margarine
3 cups chicken stock (or 3 cups water with
    5 chicken bouillon cubes)

SPICES
1 tablespoon whole cumin, crushed
1 pinch cumin powder
1^1/2 tablespoons garlic
1 pinch oregano, crushed between your fingers
Salt, to taste
3 tablespoons corn starch, mixed with ^{1}/4 cup water
    (this will be used for the roux)

1 Prepare the vegetables and set aside. Measure spices (except for salt) and place in a bowl and set aside. Melt margarine in skillet. Sauté green onion, yellow onions and sliced jalapeños until soft. Add tomatoes, cover and simmer until soft. Add chicken stock, spices and salt to taste. Bring to a boil. Reduce temperature and simmer for 20 minutes, stirring occasionally. Bring back to high simmer. Stir in the corn starch mixture using wire whip to blend into smooth sauce. Remove from burner and set aside.

PREPARING THE CHILES
8 whole roasted and deveined green chiles
    (see page 16 for chile preparation)
1 lb. Wisconsin cheddar cheese, grated*

2 Leaving the chile tail intact, slice each green chile lengthwise. Stuff chile with grated cheese. Do not over stuff or they will be too heavy for the batter to hold. Set aside.
    * Save some of the grated cheese for garnish.

PREPARING THE BATTER AND FRYING

1 quart vegetable oil
10 eggs (whites and yokes separated)
1 tablespoon all-purpose flour

❸ Add oil to a deep skillet and heat over medium-low temperature. Place egg whites in medium mixing bowl. With an electric mixer, beat egg whites on high speed until they are very stiff. Gently sprinkle in the flour and stir gently with a spoon until flour is dissolved into the egg whites. Add egg yolks one at a time, gently folding the yolks into egg whites until they are blended. Be sure not to over mix or the egg batter will go flat.

❹ Prepare for frying the chiles by layering a cookie sheet with paper towels to absorb the oil from the Rellenos. Increase the oil temperature to medium-high for frying. **This is an art; take your time and be very careful – you are working with hot oil!** Using a large cooking spoon, add one spoon of batter

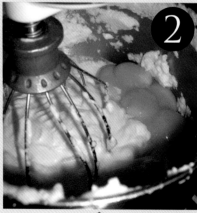

into the hot oil (the batter should have a diameter to fit a stuffed chile). Wait 2 minutes; then *very gently* add one stuffed chile onto the top of the batter. Let the chile settle on the batter for a couple of seconds, then scoop on $^1/_2$ of amount of first batter over the top of the stuffed chile, making sure it is totally covered with batter, except the tail.

5 Gently splash hot oil across the top of the chile until the batter is firm. When the bottom of the Relleno is golden in color, *carefully* turn the Relleno over and cook till it is golden. Remove from oil and place onto a cooking sheet with paper lining. Repeat the process until you have cooked all Rellenos.

6 Preheat broiler to high.

7 Transfer completed Rellenos into a glass oven-proof 9x13-inch casserole dish, placing them side by side. Using a ladle, top each Relleno with sauce, and sprinkle with grated cheese. Place under the broiler for 3 minutes or until cheese melts. Garnish with chopped green onion.

SERVING SUGGESTIONS

Serve with refried beans, Mexican rice and La Canasta Tortillas.

CHILE ROJO CON CARNE
Red chile with beef

CHILE VERDE CON PUERCO
Green chile and pork

FLAUTAS DE POLLO
Rolled Taquitos stuffed with chicken

STEAK PICADO
Cubed steak with tomatoes and chiles

STEAK RANCHERA
Grilled ribeye steak topped with Ranchera sauce

SYLVIA'S CHICKEN FIESTA
Spicy chicken tenders grilled with a medley of chiles and vegetables

SHRIMP FAJITAS
Grilled shrimp with vegetables

"*M*y recipes typically
call for the use of dried
or powdered spices
because I find these
spices bring a different
and distinct flavor to
the Sonoran style of
cooking. When using
dry spices, simmer the
sauces longer so
the spices can release
their full flavor and
accent the spiciness of
the sauce. Please do not
skip on the simmering
process; the time spent
will be well worth
the tremendous flavor
you develop."

GROCERY LIST
Beef stock
*Your choice of: beef
roast, flank steak, stew
beef or pork roast butt*
Garlic
Salt
Mild or hot dry red chiles
Cumin
Granulated garlic
Oregano
Crushed chiles
All-purpose flour
Lard or vegetable oil

Chile Rojo Con Carne
Red Chile with Beef

BEEF STOCK PREPARATION
*1 1/2 lbs. beef, cut into large chunky pieces
   (use one of the following cuts: roast, flank steak,
    stew beef or pork roast butt)*
16 cups water
1 teaspoon garlic
1 teaspoon salt

INGREDIENTS FOR PREPARING
THE CHILE ROJO
12 cups beef broth
3/4 cup browned flour (see page 17 for preparation instructions)
1 1/4 cups Chile de Sarta (see page 16 for preparation instructions)
3 tablespoons chili powder
1 tablespoon crushed chiles (optional)

SPICES
1 tablespoon cumin
1 tablespoon granulated garlic
1 tablespoon oregano
1 tablespoon salt, to taste

PREPARING THE BEEF STOCK
In large stock pot add beef, 16 cups water, granulated garlic
and salt to taste. Bring to a boil, reduce temperature and simmer for 2 1/2 hours or until meat is tender. Stock should reduce
to 10-12 cups. When beef is done, transfer to a separate bowl
and set aside to cool. Reserve the beef stock in pot. Cut cooled
beef into 2 inch cubes. Stock yield is 10 -12 cups

PREPARING THE RED CHILE SAUCE
Bring the reserved beef stock to a boil. Add Chile de Sarta,
reduce to a simmer, and add the chili powder and crushed
chiles. Simmer additional 10 minutes, add the remaining spices
and continue to simmer for 1 1/2 hours over medium-low heat.

After 1 1/2 hours, prepare the roux (see page 17).

Next, add the roux to the simmering chile sauce; use a wire whip to smooth out any lumps. Your chile should have the texture of a thick, red gravy. (For enchilada sauce it will requires more beef stock) Add the beef to the thickened sauce. Continue to cook on low 5 minutes or until the beef reaches the same temperature as the chile sauce.

SERVING SUGGESTIONS
• Serve with refried beans, Mexican rice and La Canasta flour tortillas.
• Garnish with shredded lettuce and tomato wedge.
• Great for lunch or snack burritos!

RECIPE VARIATIONS
This also makes a great enchilada sauce.

Chile Verde Con Puerco
Green chile with pork

"*G*reen chiles are used in a variety of Sonoran recipes. These chiles are so flavorful and delicious – it's no wonder cooks create dishes specifically using these versatile chiles as the main ingredient. You can use pork or beef with this Sonoran recipe; I like the flavor of pork with the green chile so I am using the pork shoulder roast.*

PREPARING THE PORK STOCK
You can prepare the stock the day before. If you chose to do this, you **must** refrigerate the stock and pork. Skim off the fat from the cold stock before using.

2 lbs. pork roast shoulder, boneless
   (if using a bone-in roast, it should weigh $2^1/_2$ lbs.)
12 cups water
1 teaspoon salt
1 teaspoon garlic
$^1/_2$ medium onion

1 Trim off excess fat and cut roast into large chunks. Place the pork into a 6-quart stock pot, add water and spices. Dice the onion into $^1/_2$-inch cubes and add to the stock pot. Bring the stock to a boil (8-10 minutes), reduce the temperature, and continue to cook until meat is tender (approximately $1^1/_2$ hours). Skim off the impurities and fat that float to the top. The stock should reduce by 5 cups. Transfer pork to a separate bowl, set aside to cool. Leave reserved stock in the pot (you should have 7-8 cups of stock).

GROCERY LIST
Pork shoulder, cut
  without the bone
Fresh green chiles
Salt
Garlic
Yellow onion
Green onion
Vine tomatoes
Jalapeño peppers
Cumin
Whole oregano
Lard or vegetable oil
All-purpose flour

PREPARING CHILE VERDE
4-6 roasted green chiles, cut into $1^1/_2$-inch *strips*
   (see page 16 for preparation tips) or $1^1/_2$ cups
   canned, whole green chiles
$2^1/_2$ bunches green onions, cut in 1-inch pieces
   (use whole scallion)
1 medium yellow onion, cut in 1-inch cubes
2 ripe medium vine tomatoes, cut in 1-inch cubes
4 fresh jalapeños, sliced in thin rings
$^1/_3$ cup oil or lard
1 cup browned flour (see page 17 for instructions)
7-8 cups pork or beef stock

SPICES

1 tablespoon cumin
1 tablespoon garlic
1 tablespoon whole oregano
1 tablespoon salt

2 Prepare the vegetables and set aside. Measure and combine spices in a bowl and set aside.

3 In large skillet heat oil, add yellow onions, jalapeños and green onions, sauté until soft. Add tomatoes, stir, cover and continue to cook until all ingredients are soft, stirring occasionally (about 30 minutes). Reduce the temperature and add the green chiles. Cook for an additional 5 minutes. Transfer the vegetables to the 7-8 cups reserved stock. Add the spices, bring to a boil, then reduce the heat and continue to simmer for 15 minutes. Reduce heat to a

lower simmer for additional 20 minutes. **The simmering process is the most important step; this is where the robust flavor of the spices erupt.**

4 Pour hot browned flour into green chile stock, and use a wire whip to blend until smooth. The texture should resemble a gravy with beef. Taste for desired flavoring at this time. If you'd like more salt or spice, this is the time to increase either or both. Your chile verde is ready.

5 Cut the cooked pork into 2-inch cubes. Add cubed pork to stock pot and simmer for an additional 10 minutes.

SERVING SUGGESTIONS
• For lunch or dinner, serve with refried beans, Mexican rice and La Canasta Tortillas.

• Garnish with sliced tomatoes.

• For breakfast, serve with eggs over-easy or scrambled, La Canasta Tortillas and Sylvia's Salsa Picante.

• Leftovers make great lunch burritos.

"*Flautas de Pollo are rolled corn tortillas stuffed with shredded chicken, deep fried until crispy, served with guacamole on top. A name more familiar to you maybe "taquitos." The name flauta in Spanish means "flute," which these delicious morsels resemble. Sylvia's still has the traditional dish, Flautas, on the menu.*"

GROCERY LIST
Skinless boneless chicken
Granulated garlic
Salt
Butter or margarine
Green onions
Yellow onion
Tomatoes
Chicken bouillon cubes
Chicken broth
Black pepper
Cumin
Salt
Corn tortillas
Toothpicks
Vegetable oil

Flautas De Pollo
Chicken Taquitos

PREPARING THE CHICKEN FOR POLLO
12 cups water
3 lbs. skinless, boneless chicken
(both dark and light meat)
1 teaspoon granulated garlic
1 teaspoon salt

POLLO FILLING INGREDIENTS
3 tablespoons butter or margarine
$1/2$ cup green onions, cut into $3/4$-inch pieces (use whole scallions)
$1/2$ cup yellow onion, cut into $1/2$-inch pieces
2 chicken bouillon cubes
1 cup tomatoes, cubed in 1-inch pieces

SPICES FOR POLLO FILLING
$1^1/2$ teaspoons granulated garlic
1 teaspoon pepper
$3/4$ teaspoon cumin
$1/2$ teaspoon salt, to taste

FRYING FLUATAS
3 cups vegetable oil
24 corn tortillas
24 toothpicks

CHICKEN
In a stock pot, bring water to a boil over high heat. Add chicken, salt and garlic. Skim off the impurities and fat that float to the top. Reduce heat and simmer until chicken is cooked. Stir occasionally. Stock should reduce to 6-7 cups. Skim off excess fat. Remove chicken and place on a plate to cool. Reserve the chicken stock. When chicken is cool, shred into 1-inch pieces, and discard bones. Set aside.

POLLO
❶ Prepare the vegetables in separate containers and set aside.

❷ Preheat a large skillet, melt margarine or butter. Add green and yellow onions; sauté until soft. Add tomatoes and cook until soft. Transfer vegetables to reserved chicken stock; add shredded chicken, spices and bouillon cube, bring to boil. Reduce heat; continue to simmer for 30 minutes.

3 Remove from heat, let cool.

4 Using mesh sieve, drain the broth. (Reserve broth for other uses – such as Mexican Rice.) Using a spatula, press chicken into the sieve extracting as much liquid as possible. Refrigerate to cool.

5 Prepare a cookie sheet lined with paper towels to soak up oil of fried flautas.

6 In a large stock pot over medium temperature, heat oil. Using metal tongs, gently dip one corn tortilla into the hot oil for just 5 - 10 seconds – just enough time to moisten the tortilla, but not crisp it). Remove and place on lined plate. Continue with all tortillas, stacking each one atop the others to keep warm.

7 Set aside to cool 5 minutes.

8 Measure 2 heaping tablespoons of the chicken into the palm of your hand and roll like a cigar. Take a serving of rolled shredded chicken and place into the center of a tortilla. Roll the tortilla into a flute-like shape. Secure the end with a toothpick. Repeat with all tortillas.

9 Increase temperature of oil to medium-high; fry 2 or 3 flautas in oil until crisp and golden brown. Use tongs to turn as needed.

10 Remove flautas from oil and set on a lined cookie sheet. Continue to cook remaining flautas as indicated above. Remove toothpicks before serving.

SERVING SUGGESTIONS
Top with guacamole, sour cream, shredded cheese, diced tomatoes and green onions. Serve with Mexican Rice or pinto beans as a side dish.

· NOTE ·
This pollo (chicken) recipe can be used in a variety of dishes – chicken tacos, chicken enchiladas, chicken burritos and chicken quesadillas – just to name a few.

Steak Picado

STEAK PICADO PREPARATION

2^1/$_2$ *medium fresh tomatoes, cut in 2-inch chunks*
2 *medium yellow onions, cut in 2-inch chunks*
4 *fresh jalapeños, sliced in* ^{1}/$_4$*-inch thick rings*
^{1}/$_4$ *cup fresh cilantro, coarsely chopped*
5 *heaping teaspoons canned diced green chiles*
^{1}/$_2$ *cup melted margarine*
2 *lbs. cubed (1*^{1}/$_2$*-inch cut) ball tip*
Sylvia's Fajita Spice Blend
Salt, to taste

1 Prepare the vegetables. Combine in a large bowl the tomatoes, yellow onions, jalapeños, cilantro and canned green chiles. Toss together and set aside.

2 Preheat electric griddle or skillet(s) to a medium temperature. Add melted margarine. Increase the temperature, and place a handful of the cubed beef onto one side of the griddle. Season generously with Sylvia's Fajita Spice Blend.

3 On the other side of the griddle or in a separate skillet, add melted margarine. Place a handful of vegetables onto griddle, season generously with Sylvia's Fajita Spice Blend. Cover to steam the vegetables, lightly tossing from time to time (approximately 3-4 minutes). When the vegetables are steamed, tenderly mix with the beef. Toss gently, adding margarine and seasoning. Cook beef until it is cooked to your desired doneness. Repeat these steps until all beef is cooked, transferring finished beef and vegetables to an oven-proof dish to keep warm, if necessary.

GROCERY LIST
2 lbs. cubed ball tip (ask your butcher if you have trouble finding this very tender cut of beef)
Tomatoes
Yellow onion
Canned diced chiles
Jalapeño peppers
Cilantro
Sylvia's Fajita Spice Blend
Margarine

SERVING SUGGESTION
Serve with whole beans, Mexican rice, and La Canasta flour or corn tortillas.

Steak Ranchera

"*A* boneless rib eye steak is tender and tasty – the perfect marriage to my Ranchera sauce. I love the flavor the bacon imparts in this sauce; along with the spices, it gives it just the right touch of Sonoran."

PREPARING STEAK RANCHERA SAUCE

3 ripe tomatoes, cored and seeded to leave
only the flesh of the tomato
8-10 strips bacon cut in 1-inch dice
2-3 jalapeños, minced
1/4 cup yellow onion, chopped
1/2 teaspoon fresh cilantro, minced fine
3/4 cup water
2 pinches granulated garlic
2 pinches cumin
Salt, to taste

1 In a small skillet over medium heat, fry bacon until very crispy. Add onions and jalapeños, and cook until soft. Add tomatoes, and cook until pasty. Add water and spices. Cook uncovered, allowing the sauce to simmer and thicken, while you prepare the steaks. Stir sauce intermittently with a wooden spoon.

PREPARING THE STEAK

6 rib eye steaks
6 teaspoons Worcestershire sauce
Granulated garlic
Pepper
Salt

2 Brush steak very lightly with Worcestershire sauce, and season with garlic, pepper and salt. Grill or broil to your desired degree of doneness. Top with Steak Ranchera sauce.

GROCERY LIST

Rib eye steak
Bacon
Tomatoes
Jalapeño peppers
Yellow onion
Fresh cilantro
Granulated garlic
Cumin
Worcestershire sauce
Pepper
Salt

SERVING SUGGESTION
Serve Steak Ranchera with refried or whole bean and calabacitas as side dishes. La Canasta flour tortillas or French bread completes the meal.

Sylvia's Chicken Fiesta

"*My* Chicken Fiesta is a medley of vegetables sautéed with tender chicken strips. I created this dish for my Mother when she was dieting; one day she asked me to prepare something low-cal, which I did happily. I put my whole heart into preparing this dish for this very special person in my life. The combination was so tasty I decided to try it on my customers. Chicken Fiesta has become a favorite, for customers wanting to eat something flavorful, and filling, yet not so fattening. I use my specially prepared Sylvia's Fajita Spice Blend in this recipe (see page 17 for ordering instructions)."

CHICKEN PREPARATION/INGREDIENTS

$1/2$ cup margarine (butter burns too easily)
12 chicken tenders – rinse, pat dry and set aside*
4 medium tomatoes, cut in 1-inch cubes
2 medium yellow onions, cut in 1-inch cubes
6 fresh jalapeños, sliced in $1/4$-inch rounds
5 heaping tablespoons diced green chiles
         (about one 7-oz. can)
$1/4$ cup coarsely chopped cilantro
Sylvia's Fajita Spice Blend

* Each serving portion will be 4 tenders per person

Combine all the vegetables together and toss gently. Set aside. Preheat griddle. Melt one quarter of the margarine (about 2 tablespoons) on one side of griddle. Increase temperature and begin to grill/sauté six chicken tenders. Add a generous amount of Sylvia's Fajita Spice Blend and cover. On the other side of griddle melt another 2 tablespoons of margarine. Add one large handful of vegetables and Sylvia's Fajita Spice Blend and cover. Cook both chicken tenders and vegetables for 3-4 minutes or until vegetables are steamed soft. Combine steamed vegetables with chicken tenders adding margarine and Sylvia's Fajita Spice Blend as needed. Continue to cook on griddle uncovered until both chicken and vegetables are toasted lightly and chicken is cooked through. Transfer to serving dish and cover to keep hot. Repeat this procedure with the remaining chicken tenders and vegetables until all are cooked.

GROCERY LIST

Chicken tenders
Tomatoes
Yellow onion
Jalapeño peppers
Diced green chiles
Cilantro
Sylvia's Fajita Spice Blend
Margarine

SERVING SUGGESTIONS
Serve with warmed La Canasta corn tortillas. Garnish with lemon, shredded lettuce, avocado slices and a fresh jalapeño pepper sliced in half lengthwise (optional).

Shrimp Fajitas

"This dish is served in nearly all fine Mexican restaurants in the Valley. My version gets its distinctive flavor from my spice mix, Sylvia's Fajita Spice Blend. I use tiger shrimp (13/15 per pound)."

SHRIMP FAJITAS PREPARATION

2 lbs. tiger shrimp, peeled and deveined (approximate serving size will be six shrimp per person)
2 green bell peppers, sliced in strips
2 tomatoes, seeded and sliced in strips
2 medium onions, cut in half at the heel and in $1/4$-inch slices
$1/2$ cup fresh cilantro, coarsely chopped
$1/2$ cup melted margarine
Sylvia's Fajita Spice Blend

1 Preheat griddle over medium heat. Prepare vegetables and combine into a medium bowl. Set aside. Rinse shrimp and set aside to drain. Add melted margarine to griddle. Add one handful of prepared vegetables. Season generously with Sylvia's Fajita Spice Blend. Toss gently until mixed with spice. Grill for five minutes. Add 2 tablespoons of melted margarine to the griddle, place shrimp onto griddle, and season with more spice mix. Continue to cook vegetables until shrimp turn light pink in color.

2 Combine shrimp and fajita vegetables together. Toss gently until shrimp are mixed with vegetables. Transfer cooked vegetables and shrimp to a warmed dish. Continue this process until all shrimp and vegetables are cooked. Divide shrimp and vegetables among serving plates.

3 Garnish with avocado slices and tomato wedges. Serve with Mexican Rice and flour tortillas.

Serves 6

GROCERY LIST

Shrimp
Green bell peppers
Tomatoes
Onions
Fresh cilantro
Margarine
Sylvia's Fajita Spice Blend

FLAN DE ALMENDRAS Y PINA
Custard, almond and pineapple dessert

CHIMICHANGAS DE MANZANA
Sweet apple filling rolled in a deep-fried burrito

"Flan is a traditional dessert made expertly in most Mexican kitchens. There are many variations of flan, and this is one that I especially like. It's rich in texture, sweet and delicious to eat."

Flan Almendres y Pina

FLAN PREPARATION
Preheat oven to 350 degrees.
12 eggs - Separate the yolks and whites from 9 eggs. Set aside.
1/4 cup sugar
3/4 cup whole milk
1 14-oz. can condensed milk (Eagle Brand)
Peel from 1/3 orange
2 cinnamon sticks
3/4 teaspoon vanilla
2 tablespoons crushed canned pineapple
2 tablespoons crushed almonds

CARAMELIZED SUGAR
1 cup sugar
1/4 cup water

❶ In a heavy frying pan, use a wire whip to stir granulated sugar over medium heat. Stir continuously until sugar has melted. Increase the temperature, and continue stirring until sugar has reached a medium brown color. Add water and reduce temperature to low. Simmer until all syrup is dissolved with water. Pour browned, melted sugar into 8x8-inch baking dish (or evenly into 6 oz. custard cups). The browned sugar must evenly coat the dish(es). Tip mold to accomplish this. Set aside to cool.

❷ In a mixing bowl, add 3 whole eggs, 9 egg yolks and sugar. Mix well, and set aside. In a sauce pan, add milk, condensed milk, orange peel, cinnamon sticks and vanilla. Bring to a boil. Stir continually to prevent the milk from sticking to the bottom of the pan. Set this milk mixture aside for 5 minutes.

❸ Using a mesh sieve, strain the milk mixture into the egg and sugar mixture. Discard the cinnamon sticks and orange peel. Add the crushed pineapple and almonds to egg and milk mixture, and stir lightly. Pour this mixture into the caramelized sugar mold(s).

❹ Lightly cover the flan with foil sprayed with cooking oil (such as Pam™). (This will prevent the foil from sticking to the flan.) Add water to a 2-inch depth in 9x13-inch glass casserole, creating a water bath. Place your flan mold into water bath. Bake at 350° for 45-60 minutes, or until a knife inserted into the center

GROCERY LIST
Eggs
Sugar
Whole milk
Condensed milk
Orange
Cinnamon sticks
Vanilla
Canned pineapple
Almonds
Cherries
Whipped cream

comes out clean. The flan should be firm to the touch but slippery in the dish. Refrigerate for two hours. To unmold the flan, place a 10-inch plate on top on the baking dish and turn over to release the flan onto the plate. Garnish the center with cherries and whipped cream. Refrigerate until serving time.

"*These delicious deep-fried burritos have been a family favorite for years – especially among the children. These chimichangas are easy to prepare, and make the perfect dessert for any Mexican fiesta. Top with vanilla ice cream to make chimichangas ala mode!*

Apple Chimichangas

INGREDIENTS

10 8-inch flour tortillas
1 can of apple pie filling
2 cups vegetable oil
$1/4$ cup granulated sugar
1 teaspoon cinnamon
$1/2$ cup powdered sugar
$1/4$ cup cinnamon
$1/2$ gallon vanilla ice cream

CHIMICHANGAS PREPARATION

1 Prepare a plate with paper towels to soak up oil from the fried chimichangas.

2 Preheat oil in a frying skillet over medium heat. Transfer apple pie filling to a bowl, and add the granulated sugar and 1 teaspoon cinnamon. Mix well. In a separate bowl, mix together the powdered sugar and $1/4$ cup cinnamon and set aside. Warm tortillas on a comal or skillet to make them pliable. Spoon 1 tablespoon of apple filling in the center of each tortilla.

3 Fold over the top of the tortilla, fold the two sides in and roll forward making a burrito. Secure with wooden pick.

4 Using tongs, place a filled burrito into the hot oil, turning over as needed until golden brown on all sides. Remove from the oil and set onto plate with paper towel to drain. Continue until all burritos are fried. Garnish with powdered sugar and cinnamon topping, and serve with vanilla ice cream.

Makes 10 dessert servings.

GROCERY LIST

La Canasta flour tortillas
Apple pie filling
Vegetable oil
Sugar
Confectioner's sugar
Cinnamon
Toothpicks
Vanilla ice cream

CAFÉ DE OLLA
A traditional Mexican coffee drink

HORCHATA
A delicious chilled drink from Guadalajara

SYLVIA'S MARGARITAS
Sylvia's signature margarita recipe

TEQUILA QUENCHER AND TEQUILA REFRESCO
Two variations of a tequila-based drink

Café de Olla

"When I travel to Mexico I always find time to have Café de Olla at one of the local restaurants. This delicious beverage is usually prepared in olla the barro (clay pots) and served in small clay mugs. This authentic Mexican method of brewing coffee takes me back in time. My senses fill with its aroma and flavor. When I make Café de Olla I use a traditional coffee pot that can be heated on a stove top."

INGREDIENTS/PREPARATION

6 cups water
2 cinnamon sticks
4 whole cloves
1/4 cup panocha (Mexican brown sugar or brown sugar)
1/2 cup fresh ground coffee

1 In a coffee pot or sauce pan, bring water to boil; add sugar, cinnamon and cloves.

2 Continue to boil three minutes and then reduce heat. Cover and simmer for 15 minutes; add coffee and bring to a boil for 1 minute.

3 Remove from heat and let sit 5 minutes until grounds settle. Serve hot.

Makes 4-6 cups of coffee.

GROCERY LIST
Cinnamon sticks
Whole cloves
Panocha (Mexican brown sugar or regular brown sugar)
Ground coffee

"*H*orchata is a delicious rice-based drink that comes from Guadalajara, Mexico. This recipe was given to me by my general manger, Mario Ibarra. He learned this recipe from his mother when he was a young boy living in his home town of Guadalajara."

Horchata

INGREDIENTS

16 cups water
$1/2$ lb. long grain rice
1 cinnamon stick
12 oz. granulated sugar
6 oz. can condensed milk

❶ Place water into a large container or bowl. Add rice and cinnamon stick, and let set for 30 minutes.

❷ Drain water from rice, reserving the water in a separate container. Transfer rice and cinnamon to blender, and liquefy, adding rice water as needed.

❸ Transfer the blended rice to reserved rice water, and add milk. Stir, add sugar, and mix until sugar is completely dissolved. Serve chilled.

GROCERY LIST

Water
Long grain rice
Cinnamon stick
Sugar
Condensed milk

"There isn't a better drink to represent Mexico. Almost every Mexican restaurant serves a trademark Margarita. This version is quite simple to make and refreshingly delicious. Omit the tequila and triple sec to enjoy a refreshing non-alcoholic drink.

Margaritas

PREPARATION OF FROZEN MARGARITAS

6 cups ice
$5^{1}/2$ oz. premium tequila
3 oz. triple sec
2 oz. orange juice
12 oz. margarita mix
1 oz. lime juice
8 teaspoons sugar – mixed with $^{1}/8$ cup water
Margarita salt

1 Place all the ingredients into a blender in the sequence listed. Blend on high speed until slushy. Pour into your favorite fiesta pitcher.

2 For a salted glass rim (optional):
Fold a couple sheets of paper towel into quarters and place atop a saucer dish. Lightly pour approximately 2 tablespoons of margarita mix onto the paper towel. Upend a margarita glass (on its rim) onto the paper towel. Lightly place the wet rim into the margarita salt; turn upright.

3 Fill glasses from the margarita pitcher.

This recipe will make 4 9-oz. drinks.

GROCERY LIST

Premium tequila
Triple sec
Orange juice
Margarita mix
Lime juice
Sugar
Margarita salt
Limes

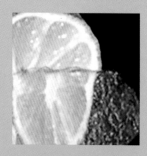

"Tias' Tequila Quencher was introduced to the Tias (aunts) by our nephew, Dan, and is one of the favorite refreshers at our family gatherings. This drink is so easy to make; you can quickly mix it by the glass or pitcher, on-the-rocks or slushy. Living in the southwest, this is the perfect thirst quencher on a hot, sunny day!"

Tias' Tequila Quencher

TEQUILA QUENCHER ON-THE-ROCKS

8 oz. Squirt soda
1 shot premium tequila
2 limes, cut in quarters
1/2 cup ice
Margarita salt

Fold paper towel and place on saucer plate. Carefully pour about 2 tablespoons of Squirt on the paper towel. Place rim of a tall glass onto the wet paper towel and lightly dip into Margarita salt. In the salted-rim glass, add tequila and ice and fill with Squirt. Squeeze lime juice and mix. Garnish with a slice or wedge of lime. To mix Tequila Quenchers in a pitcher, mix in equal parts as listed above to fill pitcher.

TEQUILA REFRESCO

A variation of the Tequila Quencher

Prepare the salted-rim glasses as described above. Using the same ingredients and measures as above, add the tequila and ice to a blender. Blend on high until slushy. Add Squirt and squeezed lime juice. Pour into tall salted-rim glass: "Slushy" Tia Tequila!

GROCERY LIST

Squirt soda
Premium tequila
Margarita salt
Limes

ABOUT SYLVIA

Sylvia Abril is the owner and president of **Sylvia's La Canasta Restaurant**, **Fiesta Catering Service** and **Sylvia's Fresh Mexican Food Products**, an integrated chain of retail businesses treasured by dining guests and party planners with a taste for quality, flavorful Sonoran-inspired foods.

Abril's family is a multi-generational staple in Phoenix's restaurant and food service industry. Her parents owned and operated the original **La Canasta Restaurant**, which opened in 1962, and remains a popular south-central Phoenix restaurant. During the 1960s and early 1970s, Abril's parents expanded the business by selling meat and homemade tortillas to other restaurants and markets. All seven of the couple's children were immersed in the food service business at early ages – and all have used their love of creative cooking and savvy business skills to enjoy success in Phoenix-area restaurant and food service businesses.

After overseeing operations in the family's original restaurant and at **La Canasta Food Products** for several years, Abril branched out and began to build her own businesses – first, **Sylvia's La Canasta Restaurant** and **Fiesta Catering Service**, and later **Sylvia's Fresh Mexican Food Products**, which adjoins her busy restaurant and catering operations on the corner of 7th and Missouri Streets in Phoenix.

Abril attributes her business success to her family, hard work, her love of cooking and paying close attention to providing quality products and service to her restaurant and catering guests. Throw in all the food know-how Abril learned as a young girl and the unique creative flair she brings to her guests' tables today and you have **La Canasta**'s recipe for success.

Recently, Abril has expanded her business offering to the Internet – offering patrons across the country easy access to favorite southwest-style food products, gift items and spice mixes. **Sylvia's Fresh Mexican Food Products** is always open, at ***www.sylviasfiesta.com***

Abril has received local, regional and national recognition for her restaurant menus and business success. She is active in numerous community groups and donates her time and products to organizations helping to feed Arizona's less fortunate residents.

Sylvia Cooks Sonoran Style is Abril's first cookbook – but rest assured, she's working around the clock on many more great ideas and great meals.

Aguacate – *avocado*

Albondigas – *meatballs*

Almejas – *clams*

Arroz – *rice*

Barro – *clay pot, earthenware*

Calabacin – *zucchini*

Calabaza – *squash*

Camaron – *shrimp*

Carne – *meat*

Chorizo – *pork sausage*

Comal – *a large flat skillet or griddle, often used to warm and cook tortillas or to sauté vegetables and chiles*

Flauta – *literally "flute" in Spanish; a small rolled, filled and fried tortilla*

Frijoles – *beans (pinto beans are commonly used in Sonoran-style bean recipes)*

Hominy – *hulled and dried kernels of corn*

Hongos – *mushrooms*

Horchata – *a cold drink made with rice or nuts*

Huevos – *eggs*

Manzana – *apple*

Mariscos – *seafood*

Olla – *a pan or kettle*

Panocha (or panoche) – *Mexican-style brown sugar*

Pata – *leg or foot; cow's feet, chicken drumsticks, etc.*

Pina – *pineapple*

Pollo – *chicken*

Puerco (cerdo) – *pig (pork)*

Pulpo – *octopus*

Queso – *cheese*

Relleno – *stuffed or filled, as in a stuffed chile pepper*

Sopa – *soup*

Tripe – *stomach or stomach lining (from beef cow)*

MEASUREMENT CONVERSIONS

LIQUID MEASURES

Fluid ounces	U.S. Measure	Milliliters
$1/8$ oz.	1 teaspoon	5 ml.
$1/4$ oz.	2 teaspoons	7 ml.
$1/2$ oz.	1 tablespoon	15 ml.
1 oz.	2 tablespoons	28 ml.
2 oz.	$1/4$ cup	56 ml.
4 oz.	$1/2$ cup / $1/4$ pint	110 ml.
6 oz.	$3/4$ cup	170 ml.
8 oz.	1 cup / $1/2$ pint	225 ml.
9 oz.		250 ml. / $1/4$ liter
10 oz.	1 $1/4$ cups	280 ml.
12 oz.	1 $1/2$ cups / $3/4$ pint	340 ml.
16 oz.	2 cups / 1 pint	450 ml.
18 oz.	2 $1/4$ cups	500 ml. / $1/2$ liter
32 oz.	4 cups	900 ml.
36 oz.	4 $1/2$ cups	1000 ml. / 1 liter

SOLID MEASURES

Ounces	Lbs.	Grams	Kilos
1 oz.		28 g.	
2 oz.		56 g.	
3 $1/2$ oz.		100 g.	
4 oz.	$1/4$ lb.	112 g.	
5 oz.		140 g.	
6 oz.		168 g.	
8 oz.	$1/2$ lb.	225 g.	
9 oz.		250 g.	$1/4$ k.
12 oz.	$3/4$ lb.	340 g.	
16 oz.	1 lb.	450 g.	
18 oz.		500 g.	$1/2$ k.
20 oz.	1 $1/4$ lb.	560 g.	
36 oz.	2 $1/4$ lb.	1000 g.	1 k.